P9-AGV-113

Chapter-1

The Diamond Healing

Tibetan medicine derives from Indian Ayurvedic knowledge, which spread to Tibet around the 5th century when the first influence of Buddhism also began to be felt in that land. In fact, Indian medical knowledge spread to Tibet simultaneously with the consolidation of Dharma (Buddhism) there. It is believed that it was during the reign of King Trison Detsen (early 7th century) that the Indian tantric Saint Padmasambhava was invited to Tibet to subdue the 'demons and devil-worshippers', to establish the Dharma and build Tibet's first monastery at Samye.

Padmasambhava is a historical figure who was renowned for his mastery of all the tantric practices. He wrote an important medical text called *The Nectar Essence* as well as other medical works. His disciple, the great Tibetan translator Vairochana, went to India and among the major religious texts that he procured and translated was the original Sanskrit medical work by Vagbhata, called *Amrta Hrdya Astanga Guhyopadesa Tantra* (Tib: *bDud-rtsi sNying-po Yan-lag brGyad-pa gSang-ba Man-ngag gi rGyud)*, which literally translates as *The Secret Quintessential Instructions on the Eight Branches of the Ambrosia Essence Tantra*. The Tibetan text is popularly referred to by its abbreviated title, the *rGyud-bZhi* (pronounced Gyu-shi), or the *Four Tantras*.

It is known that already in the earliest centuries of the existence of Buddhism, Buddhist circles in India were eliciting an exceptional interest in medical problems. According to Buddhist tradition, starting with Kumara Jivaka, the famous physician of Buddha Sakyamuni, medical knowledge had

Facing page: Padmasambhava, the tantric master from India glorified by later tradition as a Second Buddha, is said to have introduced the cult of the Medicine Buddha (Bhaisajyaguru) into Tibet.

Sakyamuni Buddha, manifesting as Bhaisajyaguru in order to expound the science of medicine.

been transmitted in uninterrupted sequence successively through a number of teachers right up to Nagarjuna (2nd century AD). Nagarjuna was the renowned author of three important Sanskrit medical works, namely, *Yoga-Sataka, Jiva-Sutra* and *Ava-bhesaja-Kalpa*. The original Sanskrit versions of these works have been lost to posterity.

Vairochana (Tib: Berozana) travelled to India and on his return to Tibet, met Yuthog Yontan Gonpo (AD 708-833), Tibet's first great doctor-saint, and passed on to him the knowledge contained in the *Four Tantras*. It is believed that in the wake of the famous international medical conference convened by King Trison Detsen at Samye, Yuthog synthesized the best of the then known medical systems and rewrote the *Four Tantras*.

Yuthog Yontan Gonpo, or the 'Turquoise Roof Physician', is a prime example of the lama-doctors and physician-saints of Tibet, an exalted and holy model of the healer drawn from the example of the Medicine Buddha himself. He is believed by Tibetans to be an emanation of the speech of the Medicine Buddha, Vaidurya (the form that Sakyamuni Buddha is believed to have taken in order to expound the medical teachings recorded as the *rGyud-bZhi*).

Guru Padmasambhava had, during the course of the construction of Tibet's first monastery at Samye, asked for the hiding of numerous texts on medical teachings and tantric medicine in various places so that they could be discovered when needed for the benefit of future beings. Hence the *Four Tantras*, which had been rewritten by Yuthog Gonpo, was also hidden in a pillar of Samye Monastery until a future time when, as noted by Padmasambhava, people would be ready to understand it. In fact, it is believed to have been extracted from its hiding place in 1038.

The period from Yuthog's life in the 8th century to that of his namesake and descendant in the 12th century, the Second or Younger Yuthog Yontan Gonpo (1126-1202) witnessed the golden age of Tibetan medicine with the inflow of increased medical knowledge from numerous foreign sources. The Second Yuthog Gonpo received the teachings of the *Four Tantras*, which had earlier been extracted from the pillar in Samye Monastery. He went to India six times and to Ceylon to

Bhaisajyaguru (Men-Lha) heads a group of eight Medicine Buddhas, who are regarded as the originators of the general lineage of medical tradition of Tibet. Bhaisajyaguru's body is blue which is the healing colour. His right hand, turned outward in the gesture of supreme generosity, holds the fruit and stem of the myrobalan plant, the universal panacea. His left hand holds a begging bowl filled with nectar which cures diseases, restores the dead to life and prevents ageing.

learn the respective version of the *Four Tantras* of these countries.

He produced a new version of the text, adding an exhaustive commentary on it called *The Eighteen Auxiliary Aids*, which was in part an introduction to the history of medicine, and which, it seems, has remained the standard accepted version to this day.

Since the Sanskrit original of the *Four Tantras* no longer exists, it is difficult to attest how much the text was revised in Tibetan, but parts of the text do contain elements which were most likely not in the original version—mention of uniquely Tibetan foods, plants, cauterisation, pulse theory, and so on. The original 8th century Tibetan translation had instead been replaced in a pillar of the Samye Monastery by its discoverer and according to author Terry Clifford 'was supposedly still there till as recently as twenty years ago'.

Over the centuries Tibetan medicine continued to grow and enlarge its field of diagnosis and application. The Dalai Lamas, Tibet's spiritual and temporal rulers since the late 17th century, gave generous patronage to the study and propagation of medicine. Initially, only monks were the initiates into the art of healing, in keeping with the teachings of Lord Buddha.

When the Great Fifth Dalai Lama (1617-82) took over temporal powers in 1642, he started three medical schools, one at Dophen Ling, one at Drang Song Duepai Ling and one at Lhawang Chog, because he felt that well functioning medical centres could come to the service of the common man's suffering. Though these centres did not eventually make much impact, the Dalai Lama himself took personal interest in learning the art of healing. He financed the research into two vital components of Tibetan medicine, the precious jewel pills and the detoxification of mercury. His patronage provided a great leap to Tibetan medicine.

In 1670 the Great Fifth Dalai Lama made a learned and young scholar Desi Sangye Gyatso the vice-chief of all the doctors in Tibet, in deference to the latter's mastery at the age of eighteen of all aspects of Tibetan medicine. In 1679, Desi Sangye Gyatso was appointed prime minister of Tibet. Desi Gyatso wrote his famous medical treatise, the *Blue Lapis Lazuli* or *Blue Beryl* (Tib: *Bai-dur-ya-snyon-po*) which is the third and most important commentary on the *rGyud-bZhi*. The earlier two commentaries had been written in the 14th century by two famous Tibetan doctors, Jangpa and Zurkarpa, founders of two schools of medicine.

Thangka (scroll painting) showing the important founders of different traditions of Tibetan medicine. At the center is Dalai Lama V (1617-82), the lineage holder responsible for transmitting the science of medicine to his prime minister Sangye Gyatso (1653-1705). The founders of the various schools of Tibetan medicine shown here, who preceded Dalai Lama V are Palden Tsoche, Jangpa, Zurkarpa and Zurkhar Ngamnyi Dorje (the founder of the Zurlugs school). By the 17th century, there was some decline in the influence of these schools and the Dalai Lama decided to institute Tibet's first medical school at Drepung.

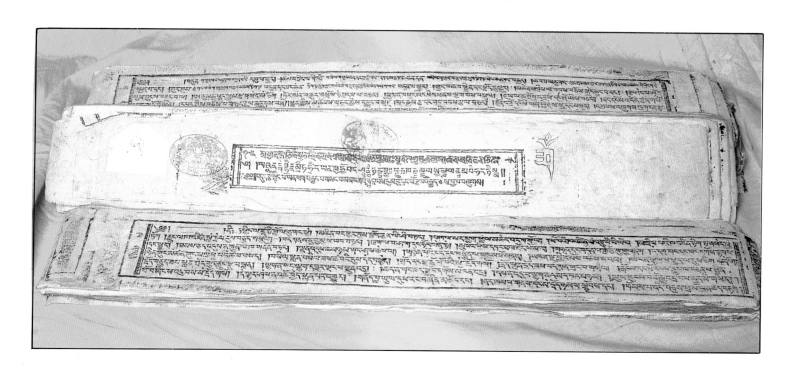

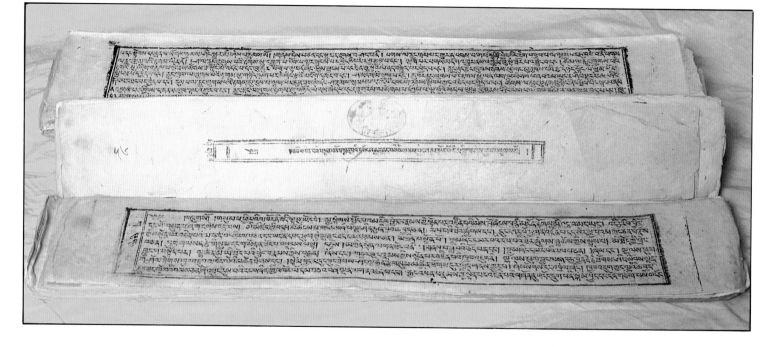

The Dalai Lama and his Regent decided to institute Tibet's first medical school at Drepung Monastery. This was followed by a school-cum-hospital-cum-monastic complex called the Iron Mountain or Chagpori, so named for the rockhill in Lhasa on which it was built. It soon gained extensive fame as a spiritual centre for medicine in Tibet (it was destroyed by the Chinese Army in 1959). The Regent declared that every main monastery would henceforth have a lama-doctor from Chagpori. This is regarded as the beginning of the 'public health' system in Tibet. Another important contribution of the Desi to medical records were the seventy-nine medical thangkas painted by him.

Facing page: Folios from a block printed manuscript (above) of the rGyud-bZhi, the most important text of Tibetan medicine. The long, narrow unbound folios are wrapped in cloth to protect them. Folios from the Blue Beryl *(below), the commentary on the* rGyud-bZhi.

At the beginning of the 20th century, during the time of the 13th Dalai Lama the outstanding physician-lama Khyenrab Norbu built the second medical college at Lhasa called the House of Medicine and Astronomy (Tib: *sMan-rTsis Khang*). Students at both of Tibet's medical colleges had to follow a rigorous routine combining prayer and religious studies with the study of arts, science, medicine and astronomy. They went on special outings to identify and collect medical plants and to be examined on their knowledge of them. It took six years to complete the entire course.

Qualifying exams for medical schools were extremely arduous and a fourteen-year course of fundamental studies was usually required before starting. Generally, it was said to take thirty years to master medicine. In addition to learning at schools, medicine was also a hereditary profession and private doctors

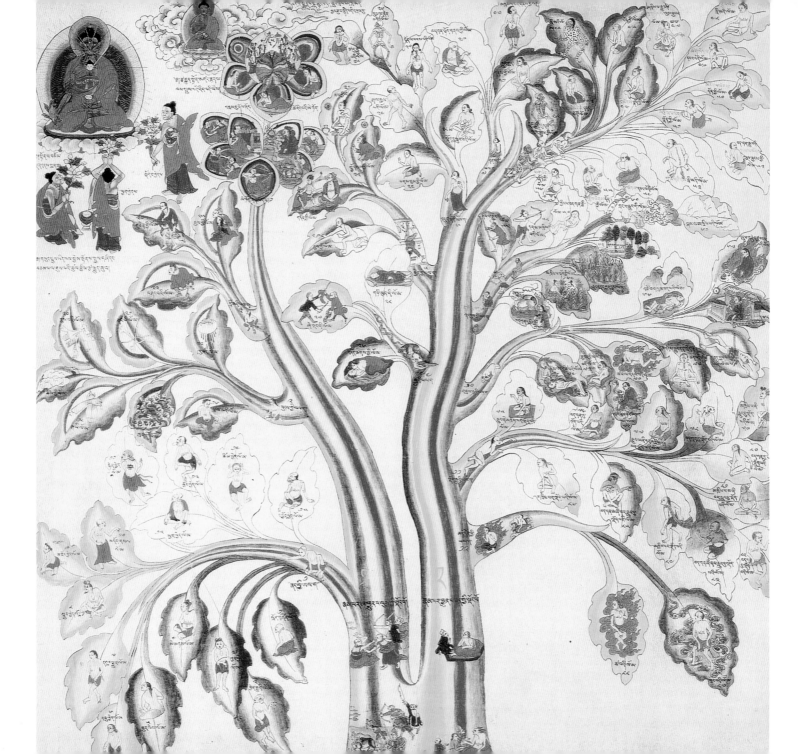

practising Tibetan medicine (*amchi*) came from hoary lineages. Nowadays, in courses on medicine set up outside Tibet, the duration of training is five years, followed by two years with a senior physician for practical training and experience.

The rGyud-bZhi

The *rGyud-bZhi* or *Four Medical Tantras* (since it comprises four volumes) is said to contain the entire teaching of Tibetan medicine. Originally brought from India, it was added to over the centuries. It is written as a question-answer type of dialogue between two emanations of the Medicine Buddha called Rishi Master Rig-pa i-Ye-Shes (Vidyajnana) and disciple Rishi Yid-las skyes (Manasija). It comprises four volumes and through its 156 chapters and 5,900 verses, gives explanations on how to cure and combat 1,616 diseases. Each of the four volumes is further divided into sections or chapters, though each of them

Facing page: The Master of Remedies, Bhaisajyaguru, surrounded by Vidyajnana, his mind-emanation (in seated posture at top right), and Manasija, the recipient of the teachings. The second painting of the Root Treatise *shows the tree with two trunks, one describing the healthy body and the other describing the diseased body.*

do not have exactly the same divisions.

The four volumes are: i) *The Root Treatise* or *Mula Tantra;* ii) *The Explanatory Text* or *Akhyata Tantra;* iii) *The Practice Instruction Text* or *Upadesha Tantra;* and iv) *The Last Text* (appendices) or *Uttantra,* which is basically an explanatory account of the first three Tantras.

The use of illustrations for Tibetan medical studies has been the main method of training over the centuries. The author of the *Blue Beryl* had accompanied his commentary with a series of seventy-nine paintings which accomplished the onerous task of illustrating the entire text. These illustrations were later replicated over the centuries and comprise an astonishing support to the understanding of the *Four Tantras.* They were intended to make it easy to teach the text to students of Tibetan medicine.

The Root Treatise explains the importance of studying medical science, how to differentiate between a healthy and a diseased body, the principal methods of diagnosis to be used and the basic categories of treatment.

The entire concept of the healthy and diseased body is illustrated in the *Root Treatise* by means of an allegorical tree. The upper section of the allegorical tree explains the psycho-physiological aspects of the healthy mind-body entity. It deals mainly with the

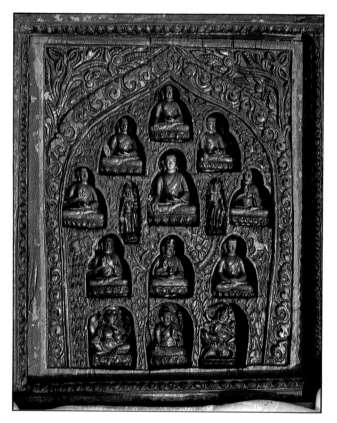

A good Tibetan doctor will regard medicines as an offering and will not make them without complete devotion to the guru and to the Medicine Buddhas. A carved medicine ritual panel shows Bhaisajyaguru seated in his Paradise surrounded by the seven Medicine Buddhas, and the two medicine goddesses ('Like the Sun' and 'Like the Moon') who dispel all diseases of cold and heat.

proper functions of the three humours *(or nyes-pa)*, that is, *rLung* (vital energy), *mKhrispa* (bile) and *Bad-kan* (phlegm).

The tree has two trunks. The first trunk has three branches, twenty-five leaves, two flowers and three fruits. The three branches stand for the three humours, the seven bodily constituents, and the three excretions. The second trunk of this allegorical tree explains the mind-body in a state of dynamic disequilibrium. Through its nine branches and sixty-three leaves it illustrates the diseased state of the body.

The first branch of the first trunk has fifteen leaves, five each for each of the three humours—*rLung, mKhrispa,* and *Bad-kan.*

The second branch of the first trunk has seven leaves which make up the seven bodily constituents as follows:

1) *Dangs-ma* or essential nutrients from ingested food; 2) *Khrag* or blood formed from the essence of absorbed food; 3) *Sha* or muscle formed through the essence of blood; 4) *Tshil* or fat formed through the essence of muscle tissue; 5) *Rus* or bone formed through the essence of bodily fats; 6) *rKang* or marrow formed through the essence of bones; 7) *Khu-ba* or regenerative fluids formed through the essence of marrow.

The last branch on the first trunk relating to the three excretions has three leaves, namely, defecation (*bShang*), urination (*gCin*) and perspiration (*rNgul*).

The two flowers on this first trunk denote health and long life while the three fruits (products of a healthy mind-body equilibrium or balance) are the outcome of a high spiritual life, wealth and happiness.

The second treatise, the **Explanatory Text,** has thirty-one chapters. It explains in detail physical diseases, behaviour, diet, medicines, medical instruments, and how to maintain a healthy life.

The third treatise, called the **Practice Instruction Text,** has ninety-two chapters, which describe in detail the causes, sub-types and treatment of each and every disease concerning: a) the body in general, b) children, c) women, d) spirits, e) injuries from weapons, f) poisons, g) rejuvenation of the aged, and h) use of aphrodisiacs.

The last chapter, called the **Last Text,** or the **Appendices,** has twenty-seven chapters and describes mainly the procedures connected with pulse and urine analysis, the pacification of disease with medicines compounded in decoctions, pills and powders and the elimination of disease with medicines like purgatives, emetics, nasal drops or suppositories. It also deals with external applications such as moxabustion, blood-letting, fomentation, medicinal baths, among others. This volume also comprises the concluding chapters of the four volumes.

Even though the exact translation of the short title of the *Four Medical Tantras* is indeed the *Four Tantras*, these are not four independent treatises but a presentation of the same medical doctrine from four different perspectives. These form the most important secular work on medicine. Other important groups of medical texts pertinent to Tibetan medicine are believed to derive from the time of the historical Buddha (over 2,500 years ago). There are texts attributed to various *Mahabodhisattvas* (embodiments of different attributes of the Buddha) like Chenrezig's (Bodhisattva Avalokiteshvara's) text on general surgery, Jampalyang's (Bodhisattva Manjushri's) text on treatment of head injuries and surgery, Chanadorje's (Bodhisattva Vajrapani's) treatise on anatomy, and Dolma's (Bodhisattva Tara's) text of 120 chapters on herbs and medicinal plants. Undoubtedly, a vast corpus of healing texts were incorporated into the official treatises by attributing the source of the above texts to Buddhist spiritual figures.

Surgical Instruments

Surgical instruments for minor operations were used in Tibetan medicine throughout, though only as a last resort. 'Last resort' methods of healing are classified as the stronger (rt-sub-che) or rigorous methods. Stronger methods include bloodletting, lancing, moxabustion and acupuncture. Rigorous methods include surgery and cauterization (incisions, excisions, scraping and extraction), though this is avoided unless absolutely necessary. Surgery formed the fourth alternative in therapy, that is, external therapy, which comes under the category of rough treatment and consisted of bloodletting, minor surgery and moxabustion. Major surgery seems to have been performed in

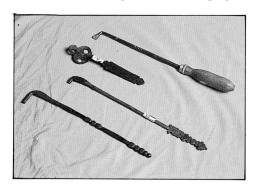 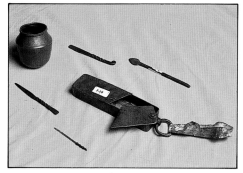 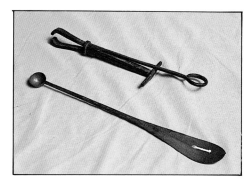

Tibet till the 9th century but subsequently it was abandoned. In the top row (facing page) are some examples of instruments used for burning or cauterization, which are made from gold, silver or iron. Below them are two types of tools for incisions, an antique case for holding a folding knife, a folding knife and last, an ancient hand seal. In the picture on the left (this page) are three types of flatirons and a two-holed instrument through which heat is applied. These are made of gold, silver or iron. In the middle is a cupping-bowl, stylets and surgical needles with the case in which they are kept. The picture to the right shows two types of long-handled measuring spoons.

Chapter-2

The Three Humours and Their Balance

The essence of Tibetan medicine has very profound roots in Buddhist philosophy. According to Tibetan medicine, there are many specific causes of diseases, but the basic cause of all is ignorance, that is, the ignorance of believing that there is such a thing as a truly existent self. This ignorance leads to the three mental poisons of desire, hatred and obscuration (or closed mindedness). These in turn give rise to imbalance in the three humours (*nyes-pa*). Desire stimulates the humour called *rLung* (vital energy, pronounced 'loong') in our body, hatred stimulates the humour called *mKhrispa* (bile or bodily heat,

Facing page: Sakyamuni Buddha's teachings themselves are a form of medicine as they look for the cause of suffering in order to remove the cause and end suffering. This doctrine did not emerge from Indian medical thought but it soon came to be associated in ancient Buddhist discourse and hence in Tibet with medical practice.

pronounced 'tripa') and close-mindedness stimulates the humour called *Bad-kan* (phlegm) in our bodies.

In fact, the teachings of the Buddha are meant to overcome the basic 'illness', that is, the ignorance of the mind, in order to understand the true nature of all phenomenon. In this way, the Buddha is regarded as a physician.

The Tibetan medical system traces its roots to the science taught by the Buddha in his manifestation as the Medicine Buddha. Like Buddhism this science was gradually brought to Tibet and it was further enriched with many regional healing practices and refined according to the climate and food habits of the Tibetans.

The innate desire of each and every sentient being to live in happiness and avoid suffering comes from our mind, but it has been said that the suffering of sentient beings

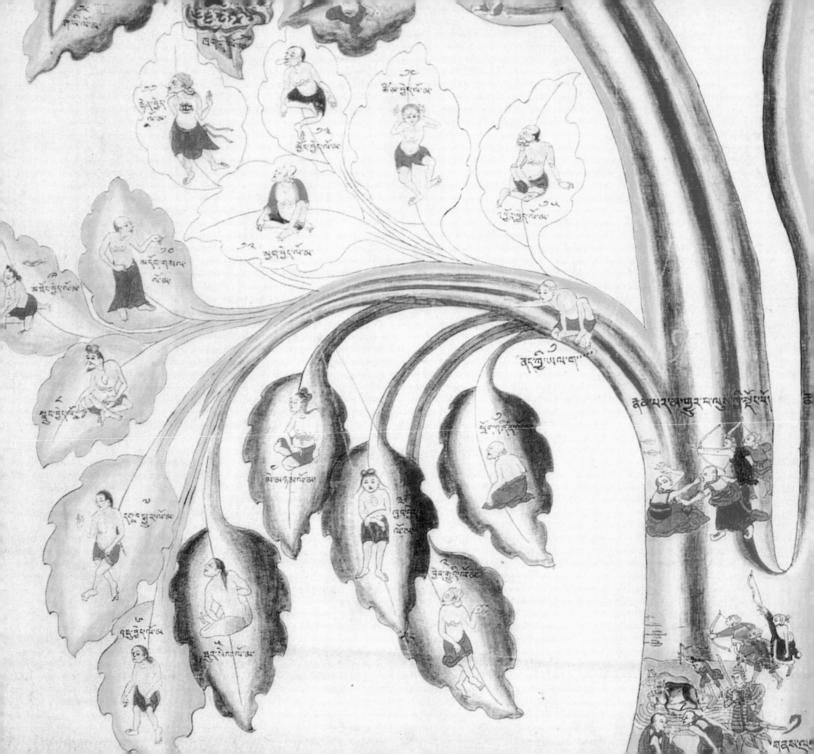

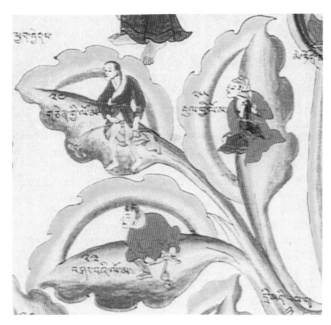

The third branch on the first stem of the allegorical tree with the three leaves corresponding to the three bodily impurities.

end of the esophagus. Life-sustaining energy also assists in the movement of the tongue when drinking. Breathing during intake of food and after is also controlled by *srog-zin*, as also the act of blowing one's nose. It also provides clarity to ones' mind and the sensory organs. If it works in a negative way, it can cause mental disorders, nervousness and weariness, making a person feel sad without cause. This Life-sustaining energy can be further sub-divided into five secondary energies, each serving as the basis for the five senses, that is, sight, hearing, smell, taste and touch.

2. *Geng-du* or Upward moving *rLung*: Located mainly in the chest, this energy circulates through the nose, tongue and throat region. Its functions are to enable speech, breathing power, as well as aiding in the functions of swallowing, spitting and so on. It gives a glowing complexion, a clear memory and physical strength. If this *rLung* does not function properly, it can lead to problems in the throat, causing congestion and blockages, which are often mistaken for a sore throat. In reality, Tibetan doctors diagnose these symptoms as having been caused by the ascending *rLung* located in the chest.

3. *Kyab-che* or All-Pervasive/Diffusive Vital Energy: located mainly in the heart, this energy moves through the entire body. Its function is to help in lifting, walking, muscular action, physical strength and growth and in perceiving or identifying objects. It helps in opening and closing the mouth and eyelids. Pervasive *rlung* is responsible for almost all the movements of the body, mind and voice, for clarity of memory and for the spirit of diligence.

4. *Me-nyon* or Fire-like *rLung*: this is located in the stomach. Its path is through the

alimentary canal but it also circulates in all the hollow parts of the body including the nerves and the blood vessels. Its functions include assisting in digestion and absorption of all digested foodstuffs, and in metabolic activities in general. This *rLung* also works in a negative way, causing liver weakness, gastric trouble, nausea and constipation.

5. *Thur-sel* or Downward voiding *rLung*: this is located in the perineal region. Circulating through the gastrointestinal tract, the large intestines, the genitals and the thighs, this vital energy controls the functions of urination, defecation, ejaculation of sperm, flow of menstrual blood, ovulation as well as the contraction and expansion of the uterus.

These energies are formed at the time of conception, after a child's contact with the mother and they control bodily functions after the child is born. Tibetan medicine maintains that once conception takes place, thirty-eight different *rLung*, one each week, are produced in the veins to form the complete baby.

Vital Energy Disorders

External factors which can give rise to disorders of vital energy are: excess of bitter-tasting food and drink; excessive sexual intercourse; lack of food and sleep; strenuous activities of speech, mind and body on an empty stomach; substantial blood loss; violent attacks of vomiting and diarrhoea; exposure to a strong cold wind; strenuous mental work or anxiety; deliberately restraining natural urges like defecation or urination.

Any of these above-mentioned external factors can cause vital energy to accumulate at its location in the body and once it receives stimulus from co-incidental factors of diet or behaviour, it rises abnormally from its site and moves to the wrong places, thus causing various types of vital energy diseases.

The most characteristic symptoms of vital energy diseases are that the pulse, specifically superficial pulsation, vanishes when pressure is applied to it. The urine becomes clear, thin and watery, and the tongue is reddish, dry and coarse. Symptoms like restlessness, frequent sighing, light and delirious mind, dizziness, humming and slight deafness, unlocalised pain, chill and shivering, stiffness in the body, insomnia, yawning, and so on, tend to get worse in the evenings, before dawn and after digestion.

A characteristic of *rLung* is that it can create an imbalance in both the other two humours, bile (*mKhrispa*) and phlegm (*Bad-kan*) as it pervades and stimulates both. It can

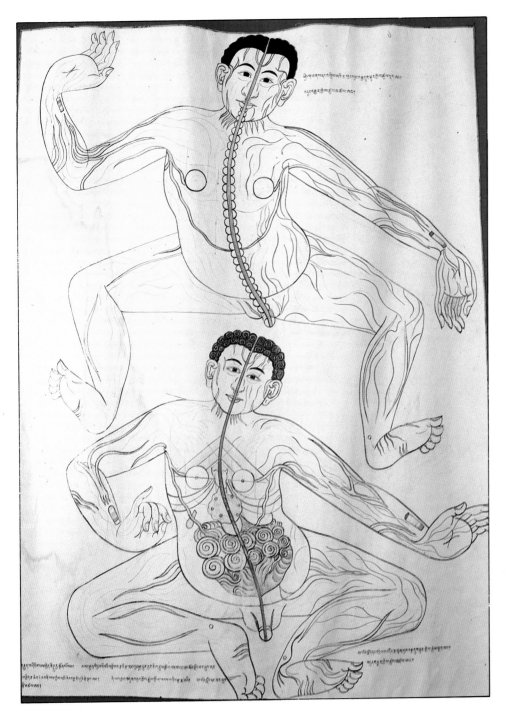

The psychic channel (in blue, left) connects the five main energy points, starting from the crown of the head and ending with the genitalia. The five areas into which the body is divided in Tibetan medicine correspond with the five Buddha families (jinas). Each jina corresponds with particular types of energies, located in the head, neck and throat, thorax and heart, lower abdomen and finally the limbs and genitalia. It is within these areas that a doctor searches manually for specific tensions.

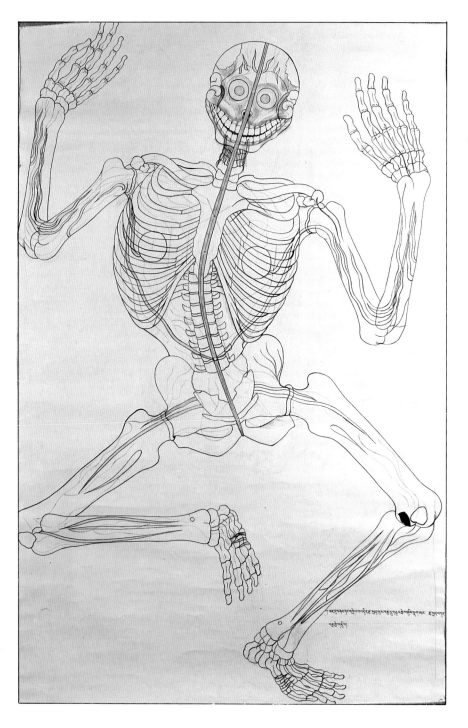

There are 189 blood vessels (including those suitable and unsuitable for bloodletting) in the body, which further divide into a series of 360 minor connecting channels or capillaries. These capillaries further divide into even more subtle channels which then form an envelope of extremely fine capillaries which cover the body and its organs like a net.

observed and then analysed, as per the hot and cold nature of the disease.

For example, if there is a malfunctioning in the *rLung*, the pulse will be found to be superficial, empty, with pauses between each beat. The urine will be like water, transparent, with large bubbles. Other symptoms will be restlessness, deep sighing, drowsiness; the tongue will feel dry, red and coarse, and there will be an astringent taste in the mouth. The patient will have a sensation of bouts of pain, cold chills, lethargy, insomnia, yawning, anger, shooting pain in the lower jaw and chest and occipital regions and dry heaving breath.

If there is malfunctioning in the *mKhrispa*, the symptoms will be superficial pulse, sensed by the doctor as thin, fast and taut. The urine will have a yellow colour, be malodorous with profuse steam. Physical symptoms will include headache, surface fever, sense of sour taste in the mouth, thick coating on the tongue, dry tip of the nose, concentrated pain on one point, sensation of falling asleep during day time, red or yellow sputum with a salty taste, dysentery and profuse and malodorous perspiration.

If there is malfunctioning of *Bad-kan*, the pulse of the patient will be weak, sunken and slow, the urine white with less smell and steam. The patient will complain of loss of appetite. The tongue, teeth and gums will be pale and the eyelids will be swollen, there will be profuse mucous production from the nostrils and the lungs, dizziness, indigestion, vomiting, loss of sense of taste in the mouth, distension of the stomach, lethargy, a feeling of being cold, and a feeling of post-digestive pain.

If the patient has all the *Bad-kan* symptoms, but all the other factors like place, season, individual constitution, age, susceptibility and the like show association with *mKhrispa* characteristics, then these are inferred as cold external symptoms with hot internal disease, that is, the first category in the four patterns of disharmony listed above.

Prognosis

All diseases may be classified as dependent diseases caused by past *karma*, imaginary diseases caused by demons, absolute diseases of this life, and ostensible diseases. These are respectively held to be untreatable, treatable by ritual means, treatable only by medication, and without need of treatment because they heal spontaneously. There are four kinds of diseases which can be cured by medicine and these will depend on internal medication, diet

and behaviour and external therapies. The most fundamental and favoured type of treatment in Tibetan medicine is modification of behavioural and dietary patterns. This is the most gentle manner of therapy and always the first to be relied upon. Decoctions and pills are for more advanced cases.

Diet

For vital energy disorders, all foods and beverages with greasy and nutritious qualities are recommended such as butter, mutton, oils, fermented barley beer, porridge with butter or meat additions, hot milk, light alcoholic drinks, and so on.

Beverages with cool and light powers are advised for bile imbalances. These include curd prepared from cow and goat milk, meat of high altitude animals, goat meat, light cereal porridge, cool water or light black tea.

To cure phlegm disorders, beverages with hot and light qualities are recommended, such as spices, honey, fish, dry lamb, barley, ginger soup, and the like.

Facing page: The third root in this didactic sequence relates to the methods of treatment. It has four stems, dealing with diet, conduct, medication and external therapy.

Regimen

In the case of vital energy disorders the patient is to be kept in a calm, quiet and warm place, accompanied by a close friend discussing subjects which will relax the patient's mind and distract him/her from tensions and worries.

Cooling behaviour is needed in cases of disorder due to bile imbalance. Patients are recommended to stay under the shade of a tree such as a sandalwood tree or on the banks of a river, avoiding any activities that will generate heat in the body.

In instances of phlegm disorder, physical exercise, a hot place, and warm clothing are needed for patients. Such patients should avoid conditions that cool the body or cause indigestion.

Since life processes depend on digestion, maintaining 'digestive heat' is important, as excess or lack of this 'heat' can interfere with the distribution of nutritive qualities from the stomach to other parts of the body.

Other categories of treatment include cleansing procedures such as emetics (which can be therapeutic in themselves or preparatory to the administration of other medicaments), moxabustion, surgery, blood-letting, hot spring bathing, and massage with oil and ointments.

Two general methods of treatment, namely, anabolic and catabolic (putting on and reducing weight) are shown above. The first strip of illustrations show ten types of patients requiring anabolic treatment, which becomes mandatory during the dry summer season (first illustration of second strip). Then we have a suitable diet and regimen: emema, purging and massage, sound sleep, leisure and happiness of mind. The last figure on the second

Treatment

strip is a patient requiring catabolic treatment, followed by the symptoms associated with such patients. The fourth strip shows cures for such diseases, specially if they occur during the rainy season: fasting, light food, strenuous exercise, moxibustion, compresses, fomentation, strong enemata and purgatives (Chaps. 29-35, Explanatory Text). This page (fig. 3 onwards) shows the diet and regimen for disturbances related to wind, bile and phlegm diseases.

Chapter-4

Tears of the Bodhisattvas:
Herbs, Minerals, Gemstones & Animals

When the tears of the Bodhisattva of Wisdom, Manjushri, fell on the earth, then from these tears was born a kind of medicinal plant. It measured one stretched hand high and had many yellow flowers. The flowers had many drops of dew on them which did not dry out even when the sun fell directly on them. (This herb still exists and is used in the making of Tibetan medicine.)

When Avalokitesvara, the Bodhisattva of Compassion cried, due to his compassion and deep feelings for the sufferings of all beings, his tears fell on the earth and sprouted a plant which is called the Tears of the Avalokitesvara. (This is a white kind of herb which is one of the precious ingredients of Tibetan medicine.)

Through the tears of Vajrapani, the Wrathful Embodiment and Power Aspect of Enlightenment, was born a dark blue kind of herb which is a bit thicker and stronger than the other two herbs. It also has dewdrops on it that do not dry.

Tibetan pharmacopoeia covers a vast range of medicinal substances. The presence of special curative herbs is one of the few things known about the culture of shamanic pre-Buddhist

Facing page: Avalokitesvara the Bodhisattva of Compassion (centre), Manjushri, the Bodhisattva of Wisdom and Discriminative Awareness (left) and Vajrapani (Chanadorje), the wrathful embodiment of Enlightenment, the three names most invoked in medicine rituals.

Tibet. In fact, it is believed that the place from which Hanuman, the Monkey-god in the Indian epic *Ramayana* picked up the miraculous herb to cure the injured hero, Lakshman, may have been Tibet. Tibetan pharmacopoeia is very large and includes plants and medicines which were not originally native to Tibetan soil, even though in actual practice Tibetan doctors normally select from a much smaller range of substances.

The fruit of the Terminalia chebula *(Namgyal or 'Victorious' arura) (fig. 1, above) is considered to be the greatest of panaceas in Tibetan medicine. In addition to curing diseases the fruit is said to possess life-sustaining properties, generate bodily heat and assist digestion. Eight varieties of* Terminalia chebula *are identified in Tibetan medicine (figs 16-23) according to their properties, viz. nectar, enriching, dry, golden-coloured, beak-shaped and small black myrobalan. Other varieties of myrobalan are also held to have comparable characteristics. Thus, Beleric myrobalan (*Terminalia belerica, *fig. 24), with its yellow fruit, alleviates diseases of phlegm and bile and those of serum and*

and bland. Their perfume itself is sufficient to lower temperatures. Yitrogma prayed to Buddha Amogasidhi that whoever partakes of these fruit may have a body that is indestructible like the *vajra* (lightning), a body that does not age, does not decay and is always firm and strong.

On the cliffs are medicinal stones like turquoise, as well as various salts. The forest is filled with fragrant scents and with the sweet song of birds. There are peacocks, elephants (whose gallstones are good for fever), bears (whose bile is good for liver disorders), and musk deer (whose musk is used to counteract sepsis and worm diseases). As for turquoise, it is said to help in every illness and thus to promote long life. It is especially useful in counteracting food poisoning and liver disorders.

The four directions or cardinal points correspond to the four buddha-fields (or heavens) of the deities Yitrogma prayed to. Lord Buddha, in his manifestation as the

Manasija (depicted in red) after circumambulating the Master three times and making obeisance to him, requests Vidyajnana (white Buddha) for teachings in the science of medicine.

Medicine Buddha, is supposed to have spent four years in a mountain plateau called Tanaduk (*LTa-Na-sdug*), the mythical *axis mundi* of the four continents or directions symbolised in the mandala of the universe. This is where he taught the *rGyud bZhi*. The four emanations of the Medicine Buddha (called Vidyajnana in all four books of the *rGyud bZhi*) impart the teachings on the science of medicine to Manasija, who requests these on behalf of the gathering in the Buddha's mythical Paradise, Sudarshana.

The seed planted by Yitrogma yielded a tree with five branches and a great number of leaves. The central branch yielded the Arura called Namgyal Arura. The remaining four branches yielded the Golden (yellow type) Arura, the Longsih Arura, the Kempo (dry type) Arura, and the Arura with Seven Folds.

The Namgyal Arura is able to cure diseases of wind, bile and phlegm, but since it no longer grows in this world, only the four remaining types of Arura are used. The Namgyal Arura is believed to grow in times of great blessings, and the present times are considered to be of great decadence. It is believed that each time a world teacher, a Buddha, comes to this world, four special things happen. The first is that the Namgyal Arura grows again. Second, a universal kind of emperor comes to rule the world. Third, the emperor has a special wheel which he carries with him. Fourth, a special kind of horse to reach the emperor to any place takes birth.

Tibetan doctors perform rituals in front of a thangka (scroll painting) of the Medicine Buddha, who is shown holding a bowl in his hands containing the Namgyal Arura, to invoke his blessings to make the nectar (*amrita*) from the bowl fall on the medicines that they use so that these take on the properties of the Namgyal Arura.

Medicines from Herbs

Great care is taken in the collection and processing of medicinal herbs. Under the category of herbs are included trees, nectarous medications (bezoar and lily), plateau medications and of course herbs. The manner, time and season of their being picked and prepared also affects their action. Tibetan doctors pay great attention to these and other subtle factors influencing medicinal substances. Such factors may in part explain why medicinal substances of non-Western cultures, when tested in the West, often fail to show the qualities which they are known for in their own environment.

Herbs should not be collected from dirty places but only from the hills and mountains, and also in the correct season. When collecting medicinal plants, the collector should not smoke or use snuff, as it is believed that the plant is very sensitive and will lose its medicinal powers. Herbs to be used for hot diseases should be collected from high altitudes and those to be used for cold diseases should be collected from low altitudes. Each part of the plant must be collected at its specific time of maturing to retain its scent and colour. For example, medicinal leaves should be collected before the flower blooms, otherwise they lose their value. The fruit is to be collected when the leaves are off the plant. When collecting the medicinal fruit it should be ensured that there are no insects in the fruit. The fruit should not be wholly raw or completely ripe. The root to

At the top in the picture to the left is a conch shell, which is used to dry out pus and cure fever of the bone. Below that are precious jewel pills in small boxes. Below these are ranged some of the important gemstones used to compound medicines. Among the class of medications which cure all common diseases of heat, bile, blood, contagious diseases, fever and poisoning are the spices and herbs shown in jars (picture on facing page), which are commonly used in households, as well as for compounding medicines.

Processed metals

Medicines can be prepared from every substance on earth, as each substance has a medicinal property because it shares in the nature of the five elements.

be used in medicine should be collected mostly in autumn. The bark or skins of plants should be collected at the time of blooming; and the leaves (and some type of bark) at a time when water is moving in the stem.

Drying and Processing of Herbs: Drying and processing of herbs is done according to the use that they are going to be put to. If the medicine is going to be used for hot diseases, then the plants, flowers, roots or leaves should be dried in a cool place away from sunshine or fire. For cold diseases, medicinal substances should be dried in the sunshine, and not in a

cold or windy place. For rheumatism, kidney and digestive problems, these medicinal substances should be dried in the sunshine. For bile and hot diseases, medicines should be dried in a cool place. If you dry the medicine on a stove and it is permeated with smoke, the medicinal power will be destroyed by the smoke.

After collection the herbs are dried and then separated for crushing and making into pills. The raw material is crushed coarsely and then powdered finely, then carefully analysed to test for quality, both by tasting it and from its appearance. The fine powder is blended

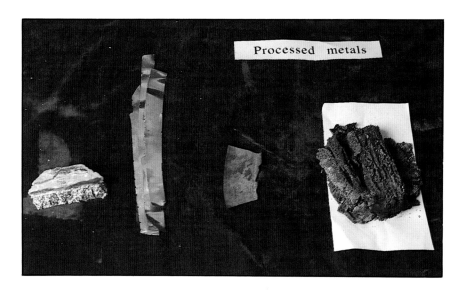

Processed metals

No substance on earth is considered vile or unfit for making medicines. Processed metals can also be used, as long as they are detoxified to render them unpoisonous.

with medicinal water in revolving barrels to form small round pills, which are coated and polished in coating pans.

Drying of medicinal plants is a very important factor in drug processing, as it helps retain the intrinsic potencies of the drug, so that it is effective for at least one year. Most types of digestive problems, liver ailments, arthritic rheumatism, thrombosis, eyesight problems and white and black cataracts can be cured solely through herbal medicines. For more serious illnesses, herbal medicine is not enough on its own and has to be administered with mineral or jewellery ingredients.

Medicines from Metals & Gemstones

As for the herbs, the medicines made from jewels also trace their origins to Buddha. To acquire this type of medicine Yitrogma had to go to the country of the Nagas (serpents). A holy man gave her a protective wheel to protect her from the poisonous breath of the Nagas. After numerous and arduous attempts,

Following pages 62-63: *Smooth shiny pills of medicines ready for administration to patients. Certain types of pills are wrapped singly in sealing cloth to keep them fresh and hidden from sunlight.*

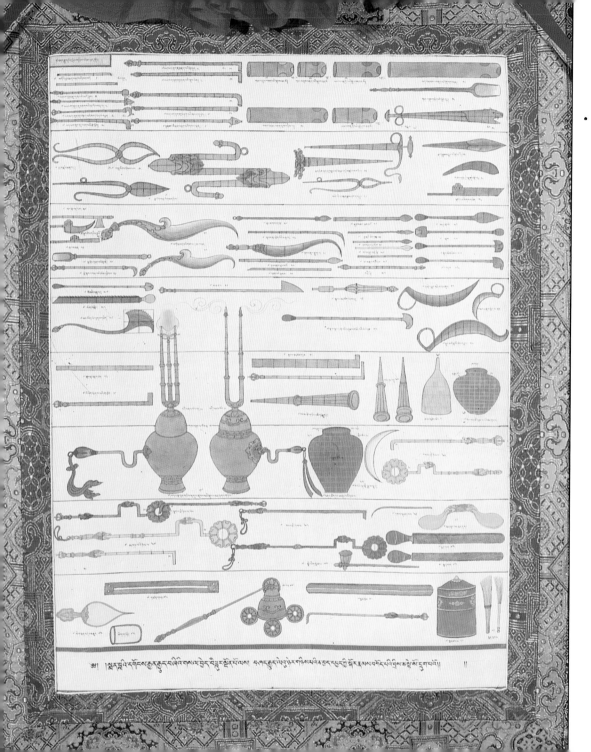

Medical thangka showing surgical instruments which were traditionally used in Tibet. Surgical instruments shown here are divided into five groups: probes, forceps, lancets, stylets and auxiliary instruments. The length of specific medical instruments is frequently indicated in the illustrations, marked out in basic 'finger-width units'.

Yitrogma was able to survive the attacks on her by the Nagas and the queens of the Naga king. When the Naga king saw her he told her that he would give her any jewel she wanted if she agreed to be his consort. Out of a wish to help all sentient beings, Yitrogma agreed to live with the Naga king for a year. She received many jewels as offerings from the king, after which she returned to the human world.

This legend in a nutshell contains the source of the jewels (the netherworld or substrata of the earth) as well as the necessity of detoxifying them before using them since they come from the land of the poisonous serpents. (Most of the jewels used in Tibetan medicine nowadays come from the ocean, or from the water.) These are regarded as beneficial for diseases like leprosy, and other skin diseases which have connections with the actions of the Nagas. These include smelted metals such as gold, silver, copper and iron; unsmelted gemstones like turquoise, quartz, pearl, conch, lapis lazuli and coral.

Tibetan materia medica mentions the use of forty-nine different types of ordinary and semi-precious stones. Before grinding stones or jewels for making medicines these are detoxified. For this, one method is to put them in water which has been prepared along with certain medicines that come from trees. This is then boiled for a length of time and the water is then discarded. To the residue is added another medicine that comes from flowers, more water and this is boiled again. After this second boiling, the pieces of stone are rinsed thrice, dried in a clean, isolated place then ground and mixed with twenty or twenty-five different ingredients, before making into what are known as jewel pills.

In Tibet, where the distances were great and the means of communication difficult, a person who lived in a place where there was no doctor used to take just one such pill to keep him in good health. It was also regarded as a blessing from the Medicine Buddha in case of serious illness.

Animals were another source of Tibetan medicine, although to a lesser extent, because of the Buddhist injunction against killing for human profit. Musk from musk deer, entrails of birds, livers, urine, blood, hairs, bones and horns of animals were used. All these ingredients were considered to be blessed by an enlightened being, by a Buddha, and hence considered fit for making medicines.

The elder gYuthok-yon-ten-mGon po (b. AD 708) synthesized medical knowledge from Indian texts and from translations of other medical systems to complete the rGyud-bZhi. *He is believed to have lived till the age of 125 years.*

Chapter-5

The Precious Essence & the Mind of Sorrow

The famous 8th century physician, Saint Yuthog Yontan Gompo the Elder, used to keep tucked in his collar a supreme medicine whose formula is described in a short text attributed to him. This medicine is called 'The Precious Essence that Removes the Mind of Sorrow' (Sems-kyi gdung-sel rin-chen Snying-po shes). This is a kind of spiritual super-medicine. Besides being effective against mental illness and various associated physical complaints, it can be· taken in small doses (one pill a day) as a super-strengthening tonic. The text for this psychiatric remedy, which has been continuously used and held in high regard for over a thousand years states: 'By giving 3, 5, or 7 pills, as necessary, there is nothing that cannot be subdued . . . especially all heart-mind diseases, insane crying and shouting, serious loss of sensibility, hiccups, a mind that grows fearful and sad without reason, big wild anger, forgetting everything, foggy vision, and

pain in the upper chest when inhaling. Especially for diseases that are very difficult to treat and for those generated by evil forces, this medicine is supreme even by just having it in the house.'

In the religious approach to healing mental illness, different Dharma practices are applied as a medicine. Where one speaks of Dharma, what is implied is not just the traditional form and practice of orthodox Buddhism (although of course it can mean that) but the heroic effort to progress spiritually out of unconsciousness and into full awareness. The Tibetan word for Dharma is chos which means to cure or to heal. The practice of Dharma is an essential means for remedying the mental and emotional obscurations that produce all harm and hence prevent enlightenment.

In Tibetan psychiatric tradition, possession by evil spirits is a major cause of insanity. Treatment in this magico-religious aspect includes Tantric and yogic practices of healing ('magic') as well as the practice and application of Dharma (religion). This is probably what has led to Tibet being known as a land of magic and magicians.

For many centuries the magic of Tibet was misunderstood and thought to be heinous heathen necromancy and witchcraft, not fit to be called religion and certainly not medicine.

This misunderstanding is no longer prevalent. Upon examining even the most elaborate rituals for exorcism of evil forces one finds that the essence of Dharma is at the heart of these 'magical' practices—in the form of compassion and the commitment to the well being of others.

The Buddhist religious healing of mental illnesses follows two approaches, the organic and the psychological.

Organic Approach: The organic approach to psychopathology in Tibetan medicine is grounded in the theory of the three humours. The three humours have associated psychological dispositions which can by various causes of humoral imbalance, express themselves as psychopathological disorders. Further the psychiatric aberrations of phlegm, bile and wind often include related physical disorders. Hence, a rising of accomplishing bile (*sGrub-byed*) can lead to disorders of the mind. In the case of *rLung*, if life-sustaining *rLung* works in a negative way, it can cause mental disorders. Dharma is at the heart of this approach also because the basic confusion (ignorance, unawareness) generates aversion and craving which causes the three humours to arise on the organic plane in the first place.

This relationship between the three humours and the three primary mental defilements expresses the basic psychosomatic theory of Tibetan medicine and psychiatry. Different treatments and medicines are applied to influence the mind through the body.

All this implies that for Tibetan medicine emotions have psychological functions. In addition the substances used in Tibetan psychiatric medicine are said to have a composition (in terms of elements, tastes) that is meant to substitute a like deficiency in the disorder they remedy.

Psychological Approach: Psychological disturbances are understood to originate from emotional strain and mental pressures, stress, problems of love, family relations, loss of possession, status of a loved one, isolation, anxiety and overwork. All these are classified in Tibetan medical psychiatry as factors which cause the 'mind to go off' in various ways.

The three defilements that generated the humours are also the three psychological forces that precipitate psychiatric humoral imbalance. Too much confusion, hatred or desire causes psychiatric disturbance. The whole psychological approach to psychopathology is based on Dharma in this way, for the essence of the arising of all conditioned existence is the development of self-centred ego and its subsequent obscurations of mind.

Dharma is not only the basis of the theory of the nature of mind, it is also a preventive medicine for mental sickness. While explaining the cause of mental illness, it also teaches one how to build a strong mind that cannot be easily overpowered by emotional strains, intellectual pressures or even evil spirits. The medicine of Dharma can turn intense suffering into compassion and wisdom rather than self-pity and insanity.

To the Tibetans a 'demon' is a symbolic term. It represents a wide range of forces and emotions which are normally beyond conscious control, all of which prevent well-being and spiritual development.

To understand the extent of force covered by the term demon, one has only to consider the famous 'four devils' who appear throughout Buddhist literature and who represent obstacles on the path of awakening. They are:

— the devil of the aggregates: frailty of body and mind;
— the devil of *kleshes:* the devastating power of afflictive emotions;
— the devil of pleasure: the alluring trap of comfort;
— the devil of death: who comes and cuts this life and with it the opportunity for spiritual growth.

Obviously none of these is a devil in the narrow sense of the word. These 'devils' like other 'demons' are outer and inner factors that exert their influence subconsciously or almost irresistibly, obstructing the realisation of higher aspirations.

These forces range from subtle, inherited and unconscious tendencies to overwhelming drives like sex, and for the practitioner they can include such demons as laziness, bad companions, dualistic thinking, hypersensitivity, increased emotions, attachment to wealth, sectarianism, spiritual pride, and clinging to tranquility. Thus, demons are primarily a psychological phenomenon associated with the multitude of mental and emotional obscurations. Among all kinds of demons,

Diseases which are commonly identified as psychiatric diseases are associated in Tibetan medicine with possession by demons. These include madness, epilepsy, stroke, plagues or infections like leprosy. Except for the last five illustrations in the series (above) which relate to causes of wounds in general, the rest show different types of mental disorders.

there are mainly said to be two: hope and doubt. And these in turn arise from the basic ignorance which grasps at the illusion of a permanent self. This ego-grasping, sometimes referred to as 'that great ghost', is said to cause all injury, fear and pain in the world. It is worthwhile quoting here the words of Ma-Chig-La, a 12th century yogini talking to her disciple:

> What we call a demon is very, very huge, and coloured all black. Whoever sees it is truly terrified and trembles from head to foot but demons don't really exist.
>
> The truth of the matter is this: Anything whatsoever that obstructs the attainment of liberation is a demon. Even loving and affectionate relations can become demons if they hinder your practice. But the greatest Demon of them all is belief in a self as an independent and lasting principle. If you don't destroy this clinging to a self, Demons will just keep lifting you up and letting you down.

Even though the belief in all kinds of personified forces of mind and nature as devils and deities pre-dates the advent of Buddhism in Tibet, Buddhism itself posits the existence of all kinds of sentient creatures in the wheel of life. Tibetans classify this wide range of forces under the one heading 'demon' which can mean forces of life and emotion that can drive the mind insane.

The Tibetan doctor must know demonology in order to perform his duties as a psychiatrist (there is no separate class of psychiatrists in Tibetan medicine). Knowing the conspicuous traits of the various demons, the doctor can recognise their presence through the patients' behaviour which reflects the demon's character. There is also an astrological aspect involved in recognising one demon from another since some are stronger during particular time-cycles.

Besides observing a particular patient's behaviour and case history, a doctor may diagnose the presence of a ghost through pulse and urine analysis. Additionally, the presence of a demon may be diagnosed by certain marks on the body.

Three key chapters in the third volume of the Practice Instruction Text constitute the main body of psychiatric theory. Although the *Four Tantras* is scattered with references to psychiatric diseases throughout, it is in chapters 77, 78 and 79 of the third treatise that we have a systematic and coherent explication of the entire psychiatric system, the character and

The primary and secondary causes of demonic possession lie in frequent engagement in non-virtuous deeds (fig. 2 in the 1st strip), remaining in fearful solitude (fig. 4), polluting, damaging and dispersing the proud spirits of ill repute (fig. 5), breaking offerings meant for deities (fig. 6), being tormented by suffering (fig. 7). From fig. 8 to 25 are shown the eighteen types of elemental demons which can cause a patient to be affected by demonic possession (fig. 26): illustrations to chapter 77 of the Practice Instruction Text.

behaviour of the different kinds of demons as well as a variety of somatic and psychological symptoms. These chapters also have an elaborate system of treatment with herbal and spiritual medicine that cure all levels of psychic disorders.

Chapter 77 enumerates eighteen separate 'elemental spirits' that cause a sudden type of insanity. These elemental spirits have peculiar traits and characteristics expressed as psychopathology in the human being affected or possessed by them. The classification of elemental spirits, and the eighteen varieties of psychoses emerging from them are:

1. *Lha* — gods
2. *Lha-Min* — jealous gods
3. *Dri-za* — scent eaters
4. *Klu* — serpent spirits (nagas)
5. *gMod-sbyin* — harm givers (yakshas)
6. *Tshangs-pa* — pervasive spirit (brahma)
7. *Srin-po* — cannibal spirits
8. *Sha-Za* — flesh-eater spirits
9. *Yi-dags* — hungry ghosts
10. *Grul-bum* — vampire ghouls
11. *Byad-stems* — evil-curse ghosts
12. *Yong-ched* — mental agitators
13. *Ro-Langs* — zombies
14. *mTshum-Tha*—ancestor gods
15. *Bla-ma* — guru
16. *Drang-srong* — sage
17. *rGon-po* — respected elder
18. *Grub-pa* — magical emanation

Chapter 78 of the third treatise deals with a kind of madness called *nyo* which is related to the senses, to emotional and organic disturbances of a psychiatric nature as opposed to the abrupt splits in consciousness listed in the previous chapter.

There are supposed to be seven causes of madness although in six out of seven cases the organic and emotional factors are the primary causes of madness. In such cases the emotional and organic disturbances are the direct development of the patient's humoural and mental disposition, unlike the situation described in chapter 77 where the elemental spirits produce sudden symptoms very different from the patient's normal disposition. An exception is the seventh case where the madness-causing demon (*smyo-byed-kyi-gdon*) acts alone.

The difference between the ghosts of chapter 77 and the demons of chapter 78 is that the former all have distinct character and behavioural traits, while the latter are more general spirits of madness.

In chapter 79, the category and manner of operation of the demons who cause oblivion are very similar to the demons who cause madness as in the previous two chapters. Only their effect is different. Whereas the demons of chapter 78 have a poisonous emotional effect, a sort of goading of the senses, those of chapter 79 radiate an effect on mental functioning, particularly the memory function—its disturbance effects a loss of sensibility and in the extreme, a complete loss of memory.

Both these groups of demons are specifically linked with organic and psychological imbalances which are the primary cause of illness in all but one case, and which permit the demons to overtake their victims. The one exception is where the demon operates alone. The cases in both chapters where the demon does not operate alone provide the basic theory and treatment of organic and psychological causes of psychopathology. These can and often are interpreted as being independent of demons since the demon is the secondary effect as a consequence of other factors.

Psychiatric treatment of mental illness includes positive inputs of diet, environment and people, breathing exercises, acupuncture, medicinal massage, baths, and the burning and inhaling of herbal incenses. Tantric and anti-ghost procedures of exorcism are also resorted to as also as religious medicine, since being overcome by demons and negative forces is specifically *karmic* (consequences which are attributed to a persons actions in the past life) even though it may or may not have psychological or organic contributing causes. Different and complicated herbal treatments exist for insanity caused by different ghosts.

Mantras (ritual chants) are also employed as therapy, and extensive religious practices often have to be done for the patient who is too incapacitated. Medicines compounded from herbal and animal extracts are used to cure psychiatric disturbances caused by harmful spirits.

Herbal psychiatric cures include medicines like the Precious Essence that Removes the Mind of Sorrow, Asafoetida, Plus Twenty-Five, the Eleven Life Sustainers and the Mental Happiness Medicine, and an incense which is put over burning coal and inhaled. These are held in high esteem for their effectiveness. Prescriptions for such medicines come from both the *rGyud-bZhi* and later prescriptive texts and together they show a vital continuation and collaboration in the Tibetan medical tradition of psycho-pharmacology.

Chapter-6

Home Remedies

In Tibetan therapy, it is the compounding of different medications which determines the appropriate antidote for each of the 424 recognised diseases. Since each herb has different potencies, depending on the part utilised, and each herb can have both positive and negative effects, Tibetan medicine is cautious in prescribing home remedies, and always advises consulting a doctor (*amchi*) so that the side effects of any medication are also taken into account. However, there are many basic herbal cures which are harmless and can be prepared at home. A few of these are given below and for each course, dosage and duration is also given (wherever applicable), so that it gives maximum therapeutical benefit. It must be kept in mind though that these are not prescriptions.

Dbang Po Lag Pa

A tonic that increases regenerative fluids, gives physical strength, and is an aphrodisiac.

Ingredients

Roots of the *Gymnadenia orchidis* (a type of orchid)

Method: The roots, with five or more tuberous divisions, must be of superior quality. Wash thoroughly. Boil, covered, in water until the water dries. Add fresh cow's milk and boil until the milk dries into the roots. Cool, slice thinly and dry in the shade. Pound into a fine powder, add equal quantity of rock sugar. Store in a cool dry place.

Dosage: Add a teaspoon to a glass of milk and drink twice daily, in the morning and at night.

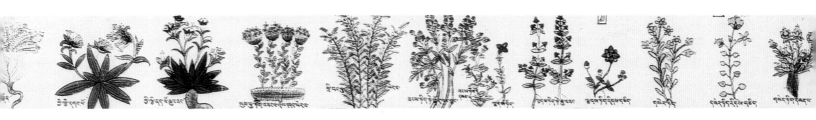

Sho Mang Tsa Ba Byug Pa

An excellent ointment for fungal infections.

Ingredients

Rumex nepalensis spreng (sorrel)

Method: Crush the roots finely and mix well with clarified butter (*ghee*) and make into a fine paste. (Best season to pick: July/Sept.)

Dosage: Apply the paste on the affected area and massage gently. Sit in the sun for thirty minutes to one hour. Repeat application for 3 to 4 days at a stretch.

Tsan Dan Dkar Po'i Nying 'Khu

A soothing lotion that prevents sleepiness.

Ingredients

Santalum album (sandalwood)

Method: Add fine sandalwood powder to cold water, filter very fine and apply or splash this water on the eyes. Its cool effect helps one stay awake.

Dosage: Apply or splash on face frequently.

Seng Lden Gdong Byug

A therapeutic face mask for removing excess oil, freckles and patches from the face.

Ingredients

Brassica alba (white mustard)	100 gms
Acorus calamus (sweet flag)	100 gms
Cinnamomum tamala (cinnamon)	100 gms
Alum	20 gms

Method: Mix all the ingredients and grind into a fine powder, add water or curd to make a fine paste. Apply on face and remove after an hour. (Caution: Avoid paste getting into eyes).

Cham Pa Sngon 'Gog
A cure for common cold

Ingredients

Cinnamomum tamala
   (Cinnamon)   100 gms
Elettaria cardamomum
   (Malabar cardamom)   100 gms
Bombax ceiba (kapok flowers) 100 gms
Gnaphalium affame
   (goldilocks)   100 gms

Method: Mix the ingredients well and make into a fine powder. One teaspoon of the powder taken with a cup of fresh curd is a good remedy for common cold.

Dosage: Two or three times daily for 4 days.

Cham Pa Bcod Thabs
An inhalation for common cold

Ingredients

Sand   500 gms
Barley   250 gms

Method: Wash the sand and heat over medium hot fire in a frying pan until very hot. Place the barley on top of the sand and inhale the fumes through both the nostrils and the mouth. This inhalation is a very effective remedy against common cold.

Dosage: Inhale as above twice or thrice a day for three days, for about five minutes at a time.

Cin Pa 'Gag Pa

A cure for a dysfunctioning bladder muscle

Ingredients

Polygonatum cirrhifolium
    (Solomon's seal)   10 gms
Mirabiis himalaica (Gandha)   5 gms
Tribulus terrestris (Caltrop)   5 gms
Coriandrum sativum (Coriander)   5 gms
Althea rosea (Garden Hollyhock)   5 gms

Method: Powder the ingredients together, add to a quarter litre of water and boil till it reduces to one-third. Drinking this decoction normalises the flow of urine, which may have been affected by bladder muscle dysfunction, kidney or urethra problems or water retention.

Dosage: Drink the decoction twice daily for as long as required.

Khog Srin Gso Thabs

A cure for amoebiasis

Ingredients

Pomegranate fruit skin

Method: Make a tea by boiling the pomegranate skin in water. Drinking this tea cures amoebiasis.

Dosage: Half a cup of the decoction thrice daily for six days.

For those who can tolerate garlic, an alternative and efficacious cure is to take one clove of garlic every morning on an empty stomach, for three days. This cure is called *Khog Srin Sgnon 'Gog.*

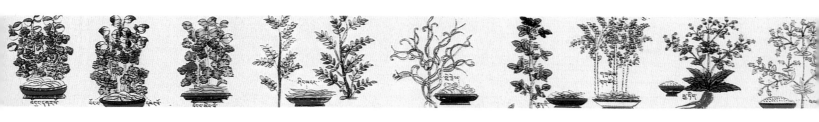

Glossary

amchi:	physician.
Ayurvedic:	relating to Ayurveda, the science of life.
Bad-kan:	phlegm, the third of the three humours.
bodhisattva:	a person who lives by the spirit of enlightenment life after life, dedicated to becoming a Buddha for the sake of all beings. *Mahabodhisattvas:* celestial *bodhisattvas* who may be considered Buddhas acting as *bodhisattvas* in order to help sentient beings.
chos:	the Tibetan term for Dharma.
desi:	regent, prime minister.
Dharma:	In Buddhism the law of the universe discovered and preached by the Buddha.
ghee:	clarified butter.
jinas:	principal centres, five in number, situated on the central channel of the body—the crown, throat, heart, navel, and perineum.
karmic:	consequences which are attributed to *karma*, a person's actions in the past life.
kleshas:	afflictive emotions or three poisons (Tib: *nyon-mongs*). In the section of Buddhist scriptures called *Abhidharmasamuccaya*, *klesha* is defined as a 'mental factor that, upon occurring in the mind, has the function of producing turmoil in and lack of control over the psyche.'
mantra:	a formulaic religious utterance, which in Buddhism is confined to *tantra*.
mKhrispa:	bile, the second of the three humours.
naga:	mythical serpentlike or underwater dragonlike beings.
nyes-pa:	the three humours that form the basis of Tibetan medicine.
nyo:	emotional and organic disturbances of a psychiatric nature.
rLung:	vital energy, the first of the three humours.
tantric:	adjective of *tantra*, a form of Buddhism, and of other religions indigenous to India, in which the means to both salvation and magical power is linked to meditation with an elaborate ritual.
thangka:	from *thang*, 'a flat plain'; scroll painting on a flat surface.
yaksha:	ancient Indian forest spirits, something between savages and elvish demons.
yoga:	Hindu system of meditation and sense control intended to produce mystical experience and the union of the individual soul with the universal spirit; derives from the Sanskrit word *yuj*, meaning to join or yoke, implying the integration of every aspect of a human being from the innermost to the external.
yogic:	adjective of *yoga*.
yogini:	female angelic deity (Tib: *dakini*).

Further Reading

Burang, Theodore, *The Tibetan Art of Healing* (trans: Susan Macintosh), Robinson & Watkins Books Ltd., 1974.

Clifford, Terry, *Tibetan Buddhist Medicine and Psychiatry. The Diamond Healing*, Motilal Banarsidass, 1994.

Dhonden, Yeshi, *Health through Balance. An Introduction to Tibetan Medicine.* Snow Lion Publications, 1986.

Dummer, Tom, *Tibetan Medicine and Other Holistic Health-Care Systems.* Paljor Publications, 1994.

Finckh, Elisabeth, *Foundations of Tibetan Medicine.* Vol. I. (trans: Fredericka M. Houser), Robinson & Watkins Books Ltd. 1978.

Khangkar, Lobsang Dolma, *Lectures on Tibetan Medicine.* Library of Works & Archives, 1991.

Men-Tsee-Khang (Tibetan Medical and Astrological Institute), *Fundamentals of Tibetan Medicine according to the rGyud-bZhi*, Men-Tsee-Khang (Dharamsala), 1995.

Norbu, Dawa (ed.), 'An Introduction to Tibetan Medicine', *Tibetan Review Publications*, 1976.

sMan-rTsis. Journal of the Tibetan Medical & Astrological Institute, Dharamsala (various issues).

Tibetan Medical Paintings, 2 vols, Serindia Publications, 1992.

Tibetan Medicine. A publication for the study of Tibetan medicine, brought out by the Library of Works & Archives, Dharamsala (various issues).

Tsewang Dolkar Khangkar, *Journey into the Mystery of Tibetan Medicine.* Vol. 1 (based on the lectures of Dr. Dolma Khangkar), Yarlung Publications, 1990.

Acknowledgements

The author wishes to thank Sonam Choepel for helping her so uncomplainingly with the translations, and Pramod Kapoor for his patience and support. The following institutions are thanked for extending all help in the photography of the items published in this book: Tibetan Medical and Astrological Institute (Men-Tsee Khang) of H.H. the Dalai Lama, Manuscript Section of the Library of Works & Archives, Namgyal Monastery Office, all in Dharamsala; Pasang Wangdu and the Organisers of the Tibetan Medical Camp and Exhibition of Tibetan Medicine and Astrology, held in Delhi in January 1997.